Out of the mouths of babes…

A collection of children's observations on life,
with original thoughts and illustrations.

Edited by Helen Lynas

To. . . . .

Love. . . . .

CHAMELEON

For Katherine, Sophie and Tim, with love.

First Published in Great Britain in 1997 by
Chameleon Books
106 Great Russell Street
London WC1B 3LJ

Text and illustrations © DC Publications 1997
All rights reserved

A catalogue record for this book is available
from the British Library

ISBN 0 233 99101 8

Design by Sally Grover Castle

Cover design by Design 23

Printed and bound in Italy by Garzanti Verga S.r.l.

With special thanks to the the pupils and staff of:
Bellan House, Oswestry School, Salop
St David's Church in Wales School
Peppard School, Oxon
Watlington County Primary School, Oxon
Cayton County Primary School, North Yorks
Filey School, North Yorks
Globe Primary School, London E2
The Institute of Biology
and
Robert Boote, Steve Turner, Janet Vaughan, Diane Arnold, Kathy Conway,
Rebecca Addis, Eleanor Sudbury, Ben Sudbury.

"Out of the mouths
of babes and sucklings hast
thou ordained strength."

PSALMS VIII.2

contents

"Well it is known,
that ambition can creep
as well as soar."

EDMUND BURKE

If you could be anything in the world, what would you be?

A shire horse -

GEMMA C, AGE 8

A boy -

DANIELLE M, AGE 5

A granddad -

LOUIS, AGE 4

A snake, so I could bite my sisters -

JL, AGE 6

a vetinary nurse -

ZOË J, AGE 8

If you could be anything in the world, what would you be?

If I could be anything in the world,
I would be an astronaut, because I
would like to be famous -

MATTHEW, AGE 9

A bridesmaid -

SOPHIE EVANS, AGE 5

If I could be anything in the
world, I would be a knight -

MARK, AGE 7

A chair so I could flip

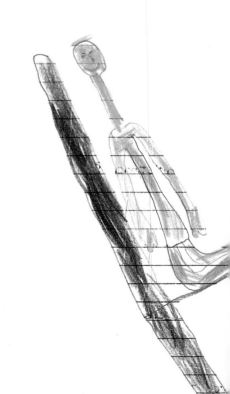

Pebbles, because I could hit someone
whenever I am thrown -

JC, AGE 6

A squirrel, so I could climb up trees and
spy on people and if they were doing
anything bad I could go down and scratch
them with my sharp nails -

THOMAS PYM, AGE 6

A rabbit, so I
could bounce
around -

BESS, AGE 6

I would be a
Labrador -

SEBASTIAN, AGE 6

I want to be a dinner lady -

SHARMINA B, AGE 7

Myself with a better haircut -

TOM, AGE 10

A Little Chef
waiter -

JOHN, AGE 8

people over backwards -

LEO EMMETT, AGE 6

I would be a cheetah, so I could eat when I
want -

PETER D, AGE 9

I would be a bird and fly over rain
forests, and when someone gets a gun
I would turn into a man -

GAETAN, AGE 10

A hedgehog, so
I can live in the forest -

MICHELLE, AGE 7

A forest for nature -

STEPHEN, AGE 7

If you could be anything in the world, what would you be?

If I could be anyone in the whole world, I would still be myself because I would miss my family -

CHARLOTTE, AGE 9

I would like to be a bug -

TOM, AGE 7

At home -

PETER J, AGE 8

I want to be a ghost and haunt a house -

CAROL E, AGE 10

I would like to be a deer

I would be someone that helps very poorly people -

SALLY, AGE 9

I would like to be a rabbit so people could stroke me -

HAYLEY, AGE 6

If I could be anything, I would be an apple tree because people could pick my apples and sit in my branches -

KATHERINE L, AGE 9

If I could be anything in the world, I would be the strongest man on earth -

SAM, AGE 8

A Japanese judo player -

SUSI J, AGE 8

If I could be anything in the world, I would like to be someone's royal daughter, then I could get anything I could wish for -

LATIFA B, AGE 9

nd give people rides -

NICOLE, AGE 6

I would rather be the blue sea -

SALMAH O, AGE 10

If I could be anything in the whole world, I would be an accountant -

MAY H, AGE 10

I want to be a grown-up -

RAHUL M, AGE 6

"Children begin by loving their parents.
After a time they judge them.
Rarely, if ever, do they forgive them."

OSCAR WILDE

What is the best thing about mums and dads?

She cuddles me if I fall over, and puts on plasters and cream -

SARAH SMITH, AGE 6

She does the cooking and vacuuming -

ZARA, AGE 4

Dads get rid of mums' head lice -

POSIE, AGE 7

She works to get money to pay for the house -

LEO EMMETT, AGE 6

I like giving my mummy flowers It makes me happy when my mummy is happy

PHOEBE BALL, AGE 5

Chips and pie -

RYAN L, AGE 5

They make food for you -

THOMAS PYM, AGE 6

The best thing about my mum and dad is that I can talk to them about things -

EMILY, AGE 10

12 | 13

What is the best thing about mums and dads?

She cares for me and is a loving mum -
NATALIE, AGE 10

The best thing about my mum and dad is they let me try everything unless they have a really good reason -
HELEN, AGE 10

They give you hugs -
JENNY WONG, AGE 6

He always burns the toast -
LAURA, AGE 6

They give you baths -
HANNAH-MAY ELMASRY, AGE 6

My dad is my favourite person. I like him because he is a bit like me -
TOM, AGE 10

They feed you and

She loves me -
JAMES, AGE 7

My mum is the best mum in the world. She is kind and makes up for my dad not being there. She is wonderful -
KATY, AGE 10

They go to work -
DAVID JANES, AGE 5

They are happy and smiley -
AYODELE A, AGE 9

I think they loo

My mum is friendly and kind but sometimes gets very angry. My dad is nice and makes jokes, but always asks me to wash up -
MARIE, AGE 10

The best thing about mums is that they have children and love them and care for them -

CHLOË PARKER, AGE 7

She tucks me into bed -

JAMES, AGE 5

My dad gives piggy backs -

CATHERINE WIGNALL, AGE 5

When she smacks me, she cuddles me -

- GEORGE H, AGE 4

Dads go at 100 mph -

POSIE, AGE 7

He likes to have breakfast -

MILLIE, AGE 4

give you water -

JOANNA LATHAM, AGE 6

When they come back with the newspapers, they have bought you sweets -

GEORGINA, AGE 6

He makes funny faces -

RHIANNON D, AGE 4

Dads fix things -

SARAH SMITH, AGE 6

He throws me up when he comes home from work -

LEO EMMETT, AGE 6

rtet us.

The best thing about mum is when you ask her for some money she always gives me some out of her purse. The good thing about dad is he sometimes brings sweets home from work. But the bad thing is I have to do tables every night (I mean, how bad can you get?) -

NAOMI, AGE 10

"If a child annoys you,
quiet him by brushing his hair.
If this doesn't work, use the other
side of the brush on the other
end of the child."

ANON

What does your mum or dad do that annoys you most?

Mum and Dad annoy me when I get downstairs at night and find they've gone

PIP S-S, AGE 8

I hate it when mum and dad get my report -

OLIVER O, AGE 8

They are OK, but the things that annoy me are my mum singing and my dad going to the toilet too long -

SARA, AGE 11

Your'e room's a disgrace!

Have you got any homework?

Go straight upstairs

Hurry up and eat your tea!

what did you do at school today?

JANE S, AGE 9

My mum thinks she is a handyman -

KAYLEIGH, AGE 9

My dad is awful. He shows off, and mummy pretends she is in James Bond or something awful like that -

ANON

16 | 17

What does your mum or dad do that annoys you most?

The most annoying thing is when there is a programme on and they have been talking, then when we talk it's 'Sssh' all the time -

SAM, AGE 10

When they say I'm not allowed to swing from the shed roof -

TIM P, AGE 10

There is nothing bad about them, but when they yell at each other it annoys me -

CLAIRE, AGE 11

My dad annoys me bea

What really annoys me is when they drag us off to a stately home -

ADAM, AGE 10

When I walk past my dad he slaps me on the head, and when my mum does the ironing she puts on music and dances -

STEVEN K, AGE 10

The thing that my mum and dad do that annoys me most is calling me Princess in front of my friends, and all other in barising things like that -

LORRAINE B, AGE 8

Mum and dad are kind and nice but they always get their own way -

GINNY, AGE 10

They can be very nice, but sometimes I feel like swearing at them if they are not sympathetic, and they accuse you about being late when they told you to do the thing that made you late -

RACHAEL D

My mum anoys me when she says something about makeing up my mind, and she dose it for me -

SAM, AGE 10

When they agree something with me and then it doesn't happen -

JESSICA, AGE 7

aUse he bUrps so loUd –

ELEANOR, AGE 7

My dad annoys me when he eats - his jaw clicks like mad -

TOM, AGE 10

They ask questions -

HARRY, AGE 7

They say I have to eat up all my tea when I've already had it -

EMMA B, AGE 10

My mum brings home lots of children to our house, but although it is kind for their parents it sometimes annoys me -

JENNY, AGE 10

18 | 19

"True knowledge
lies in knowing how
to live."

BALTASAR GRACIÁN

What should be banned from school, and why?

I think Eglish should be band -

GEMMA C, AGE 8

Play, because I like to work -

HUGO, AGE 6

BEN P, AGE 9

Work should be banned from school so we could play all day -

GAETAN, AGE 10

Sweets, because it makes your teeth go wobbly -

SIMON, AGE 6

Videos, because my dad said we should be working instead -

HANNAH, AGE 6

I think school uniform, because we keep having to tackle the top button -

TOM, AGE 7

Pulling wallpaper off in the dining room, because if they do then more wallpaper needs to be put up -

HUGH, AGE 6

What should be banned from school, and why?

You mustn't be silly, because it is dangerous -

RAJU R, AGE 8

Assembly, because it is so boring -

REESE, AGE 8

I think hard work should be banned, because we never finish it, and we have to do that work and today's work as well -

MARIA P, AGE 9

Bangles and marbles, because any little one can put them in their mouth and get hurt a lot -

LOUISE, AGE 8

Naughty children, because they

Bullying should be banned from school, because it hurts people -

DAVID L

Teachers should be banned from school, because they are boring but nice -

SHONA, AGE 10

Uniforms are boring. We should only wear them on school trips in case we get lost -

CHARLOTTE, AGE 10

Racism, because too many people are racist and you get hurt and angry and it starts fights -

NICK A, AGE 10

Head teachers, because nobody likes them -

STEPHEN, AGE 9

Racism, fighting, and bullying should be banned, because I think it is destroying the school and people are getting hurt -

TANIA U

Pens, because they can fall and hit someone on the head with the sharp bit -

PETER, AGE 6

give the teachers poorly throats -

ALISON, AGE 6

School runners, because they just get lost and you can't find them -

RUTH O

DANGER
VERY SHARP PENCILS

Head teachers should be banned, because they just tell you off for the fun of it -

DEBORAH, AGE 10

Even very young children need
to be informed about dying. Explain the
concept of death very carefully to your child.
This will make threatening him with
it much more effective.

P.J. O'ROURKE

What makes you frightened?

I get frightened when I get out of bed at night and go to the loo and it's all black and dark -

SARA, AGE 11

The thought of one day being abducted by aliens scares me -

LIZZIE, AGE 10

I like films with shooting and blood, but sometimes some of them scare me and make me frightened -

MARIE, AGE 10

RICHARD K, AGE 8

The dark makes me frightened because I think someone is going to jump out at me -

GINNY, AGE 10

When I am reading in front of assembly, because I am shy -

ALEX B

I'm frightened of the sky falling on my head -

PETER L, AGE 6

The things that make me frightened are earthquakes and wars that might start where I am, because with earthquakes the ground sometimes splits and I might fall into it. The reason I am frightened of a war starting is if someone I know dies, or I might die -

HELEN, AGE 10

I get frightened by ghosts and poltergeists and the ozone layer going -

RACHAEL D

What makes you frightened?

I would be frightened if I was in a room full of scorpions and the door was locked -

TRISTAN, AGE 8

I get frightened when I go for a walk in the woods with my friends, but I'm too scared even to tell them -

MARIE L, AGE 10

I get frightened when I lay in bed and see black shadows made out of clothes and balls, and I think they are humans just watching me -

JENNY, AGE 10

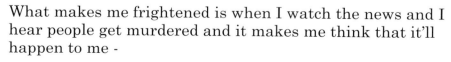

Caterpillars make me feel frig

I get scared if I think I'm going to get embarrassed somehow -

GLYN M

AAAH...

I am going to kill you

CAROLINE, AGE 7

What makes me frightened is when I watch the news and I hear people get murdered and it makes me think that it'll happen to me -

FRANK, AGE 8

When the big ones bump into me -

CHLOË, AGE 7

I am frightened at night when the lights are off and it's really dark, because I hear horrible noises and there are horrible shadows at my window -

EMMA, AGE 7

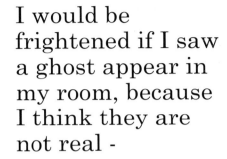

I would be frightened if I saw a ghost appear in my room, because I think they are not real -

ANDREW, AGE 10

Soldiers, because they look scarey -

DANIEL, AGE 7

ened, because they are saggy -

CHI-WAI, AGE 9

Being lonely -

BEN, AGE 7

Two things that make me frightened are the thought of my house burning down, because I like my house, and dying, because it means your life is up -

EMILY, AGE 10

"Her vocabulary was as bad
as, like, whatever."

(UNKNOWN)

Children are never lost for words, even if it involves creating their own special blend of spelling, grammar and dialect. Decode the language and the meaning shines through even more richly. 'Gronups' find them endearing, but to avoid embarrassment, the names of the originators have been withheld.

The Queen makes all the lures and al the disishons for Britan.

What do you think about kissing?
It is discoscen.

The queen makes lots of spechis and dose lots of riding and has very nice jurlrey.

What do you think about grandparents?
My gran perents Spoil me and let me go eny where I want. I thinc my gran is verey cind and I wold uprishet what she did for me.

What do you want to be when you grow up?

I wolde be a plaice because I colde cach bugler's.

A close disina.

I want to be a proffeshnel footbaler.

A hear dresa becoas it is good.

I wode by a shop a sistens in a sweat shop.

"Birds in their little nests agree;
And 'tis a shameful sight,
When children of one family
Fall out, and chide, and fight."

ISAAC WATTS

What do you like, or dislike about sisters and brothers?

Her nappy smells -
EDWARD, AGE 5

I like it when she hugs me -
CAMILLA, AGE 5

I like her new remote-control car -

HUGH, AGE 6

I like everything about my sister Sammy, and I do like everything about my sister Sammy -

SARAH, AGE 7

I am sharing sweets with my sister and she is sharing her teddy bear. God wants people to be nice to each other and share.

Catriona Till

I'd love to have a sister so I could rip up all her Barbies -
GWILYM, AGE 7

I don't like sisters when they argue with you because they are meant to respect their older brothers and sisters -
RYAN, AGE 10

I like my sisters. Well, you have to like them somehow as they've got the same blood as you -

LUCY, AGE 11

What do you like, or dislike about sisters and brothers?

She is ugly and bossy and gets everything she wants -

NAME WITHHELD (to save the writer from a battering)

Peter is a pain in the neck -

CARMEN, AGE 7

I like them because they listen -

THOMAS, AGE 7

They are fun and they're naughty -

CHLOË, AGE 7

I like my big brother because he

I like my brother because when you are sad you can go and talk about how sad you are to him -

ROSIE L, AGE 7

You can play Barbies together -

EMILY, AGE 7

I like them because they are fun to argue with. They can very rarely help you, and they give you their old pop tapes. They also recommend stuff for you -

CHLOË, AGE 10

I don't like my brother because he cries a lot and gets me into trouble, but he's fun to play with -

SAM W, AGE 10

My brother tells my mum and dad I hit him when he hit me! -

RACHEL, AGE 10

They kick, fight and swear -

GLEN, AGE 7

ils my bike for me sometimes —

EDWIN, AGE 6

They are useful when I'm bored because they play with me, but they always tease and fight -

ANNA, AGE 10

I don't like little ones because they bite you but I do like them when they're more grown up -

JAMES, AGE 7

"The best way to make children good is to make them happy."

OSCAR WILDE

What makes you happy?

Smiles -

AYODELE A, AGE 9

Dad and Mum -

NATASHA, AGE 4

Me and my friend are in the field picking flowers for each other. It makes me feel happy.

ANON

When mummy kisses me -

TOMAS GONZALEZ, AGE 6

Lloyd squealing and mum and dad tickling me and my uncle playing tricks on me -

JACK, AGE 7

Doing science a lot and getting a good brain -

FOYERS, AGE 10

It makes me happy when my sister cuddles me and when I go to gran and grandpa's -

ALICE M, AGE 8

What makes you happy?

When the teacher tells me that I don good work -
HUSHARA B

A new baby sister -
LUCKY K, AGE 9

Ladies -
DANIELLE M, AGE 5

I'm happy when I can play outside in the woodland with my friends from next door -
MARIE L, AGE 10

When your pet dies and you get a new one -
BEN, AGE 6

When people smile -
SHANAN A, AGE 8

My dad makes me happy because he is always funny -
NICK, AGE 10

Having friends that like you and care for you, ha

When someone is proud of me -
ASHRAFUL, AGE 10

The poor getting a home -
PETER B, AGE 7

If my mum did not have asthma that would make me happy, and her too -
KELLY T, AGE 10

My mum and dad and melissa and my dog and alex make me happy -
MARC Z, AGE 8

I can never really be very happy because my cat Boris will never be there again, and he always made me happy -
CLAIRE, AGE 10

Holiday with horses would make me very happy, or getting wet in the rain forests with the rain from the leaves -

SAM, AGE 10

Pocket money every week -

MURYA S, AGE 11

The thing that makes me happy is when my brother finds another house -

KERRY, AGE 10

What makes me happy is going out with my parents, because I know it is going to be good -

ANDREW, AGE 10

ng a family that loves you and gives you things -

AMANDA, AGE 10

People who laugh at me, because they think I am funny make me happy -

FRANCESCA R, AGE 9

I'm happy when I get sweets off my mum (that's rare) -

TOM, AGE 10

When dad gets home from work early as a surprise -

VIVIENNE, AGE 6

"Pretty much all the
honest truth telling in the world
is done by children."

OLIVER WENDELL HOLMES

What do grown-ups do to have fun?

They play hide and seek with little children -
SARAH SMITH, AGE 6

ELLIE, AGE 9

Sit by the river and have a picnic.
They have sandwiches and apple juice -
EMMA COX, AGE 6

Tell jokes to other grown-ups - special grown-up jokes. Then they laugh. I tried to listen once, but I could not hear the words -
CATHERINE WIGNALL, AGE 5

Go next door and have a cup of tea -
DANIEL R, AGE 7

Cook -
ANNABELLE, AGE 4

Drink in the pub and have hugs -
KAREN, AGE 7

What do grown-ups do to have fun?

They watch films, chat and tell mysterious stories -

SALMAN O

They get sexy -

MAX, AGE 6

They smoke. I'm not going to smoke. I know it is yuk because I can tell by the smell -

DELPHINE, AGE 9

Talk and go to work -

KRISTIAN, AGE 4

Lie on the sofa -

SAM ROBERTS, AGE 5

Grown-ups have fun doing shopping and buying things -

LOUISE W

Cut lawns and strimming -

TOM, AGE 4

Mummy likes diving. Daddy likes to sit in a deck chair -

HARRY WROUGHTON-CRAIG, AGE 5

They win the national lottery -

JACK, AGE 10

My mum and dad would paint the house for fun -

ALUN, AGE 7

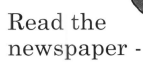

Read the
newspaper -
HUGO, AGE 6

Grown-ups sit
around drinking
cups of coffee in
their spare time -
JASMINE

A tape from the
'60s and a cup of
coffee - that's the
way grown-ups
have fun -
DEBORAH. AGE 10

They talk a lot, that is their
fun -
SARAH, AGE 7

Un in the nit -
ZOË S

Tell children off -
CLAIRE L, AGE 7

Not a thing. They
just sit down -
MICHELLE, AGE 7

They sit on the sofa and drink cups of tea
while watching *The Adventures of Tintin* -
RACHEL, AGE 10

Grown-ups like long sleeps and having a
lie-in in the morning. They like to see old
friends, and having a warm cup of tea. I
think they also like going to parties -
CHLOË, AGE 10

Go to bed -
SIAN, AGE 10

They like
telephoning -
MARK P, AGE 6

"To be good is noble, but to
teach others how to be good is nobler -
and less trouble."

MARK TWAIN

What do you think about teachers?

I hate them. But my last few have been okay and I am sure that the next few will be -

EMMA, AGE 11

I hate it when they give me homework. When I get home I blow a fuse -

KATIE D, AGE 8

Well, it depends really. They have a job to do, but some teachers could be happier -

SAM, AGE 11

They are horbol -

JAYDEN, AGE 7

I like teachers because they teach us -

JACK, AGE 7

They do keep on -

ABDUL B, AGE 10

I like teachers wene tahe give me Eglish -

MATTHEW A

All they ever do is teach you - it is boring-

FATHEHA, 10

What do you think about teachers?

They're mainly all right but they have their annoying moments -

SAM, AGE 10

I feel sorry for them -

JAHANGIR H

Some teachers are okay, some teachers are mean, and some teachers are disgusting -

STEVEN, AGE 10

They are very good, because even when they tell you off they are thinking about your education -

BETH, AGE 11

 They are the worst

I suppose they are only doing their job -

CLAIRE, AGE 10

Teachers are nothing but hard work -

SHAMI, AGE 10

They are boring, some are ugly, annoying and smelly -

TIM, AGE 9

They are repulsive toads turned into humans -

SCOTT, AGE 10

Teachers must have an awful lot of patience to put up with us lot for five days of the week -

EMILY, AGE 10

They are annoying people who make you work and are strict, and are lethal with their meter stick -

GLYN

They make you write things to go in a public book when you don't want it in there -

ALEX, AGE 10

They are there to annoy us, but they deserve higher pay anyway. They are captured and tortured until they agree to be a teacher -

MAX, AGE 9

thing on earth -

PETER L

Ruthless -

ROBERT C

You can cuddle them -

BEN, AGE 6

They are good. Then again, they are bad. I will tell you later -

NAZIA

They are nice people to be around -

ERIN, AGE 7

Education is the period
during which you are being instructed
by somebody you do not know,
about something you do not
want to know.

G.K. CHESTERTON.

What is the best thing about school? Why do we have to go there?

To learn the truth -
EMMA, AGE 6

So you can learn to play nicely in the playground -
ALEXANDER, AGE 6

I like having my milk -
LUCY, AGE 4

Because it is fun! -
SOPHIE EVANS, AGE 5

I like my packed lunch -
HANMORE, AGE 5

So your mums and dads can work -
STEPHEN, AGE 4

Because they do the register -
RYAN LEE, AGE 5

My friends -
RHYS W, AGE 6

You have to learn numbers and painting and be clever and eat your dinner -
JADE N, AGE 5

Because mum tells me -
KEVIN R, AGE 5

Sausages and fish at lunch time -
KOLBEINN M, AGE 6

well done ellie

ELLIE, AGE 9

Going home -
KATHERINE, AGE 7

"Men are but children
of larger growth."

JOHN DRYDEN

What does the
Prime Minister do?

He sits at a big desk in 10
Downing Street worrying
about the next election -

ALICE MALIN, AGE 7

The Prime Minister gose around the world
having parties and talking about money -

TOM, AGE 10

ALICE M, AGE 7

What does the Prime Minister do?

The Prime Minister tries to run things and sometimes succeeds, but I think we shouldn't let Prime Ministers rule so many things and rule our own ways ourselves -

CATHERINE, AGE 11

I have no idea what the Prime Minister does. You always see him on television arguing with other people. He's not that important really -

SIMON, AGE 10

He makes up the rules as he goes along -

AMY, AGE 9

The Prime Minister can be good at times, but I don't think he does much apart from cause confusment in parlement -

JENNY, AGE 10

He does nothing much but lays around an

The Prime Minister walks around everywhere in a nice suit complaining -

JANEY, AGE 9

The prime minister m to follow

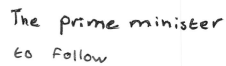

He helps us a lot because someone has to make the rules, don't they? -
RHIANNON, AGE 9

I think the Prime Minister stands in court and does business -
NICOLA, AGE 10

The Prime Minister just drinks beer and has a government party -
ANON

The Prime Minister argues with other Prime Ministers -
SAMANTHA B, AGE 9

Eats, goes to the toilet, bosses people around -
SCOTT, AGE 10

He prays to God -
MARC Z, AGE 8

He rules the world -
KHALEDA K

tuffs himself with chocolate biscuits -
FRANCIS, AGE 9

He fixs wot is bracan -
SAM, AGE 6

He goes blah blah de blah -
JAYDEN, AGE 7

rules for everyone else

r steel

The Prime Minister looks after the country he lives in so he can make it better -
ANDREW, AGE 10

What does the Prime Minister do?

The Priminister argues for different silly rights which I don't think concerns me -

SAM, AGE 10

I think the Prime Minister is very important but has an extremely boring life and I really wouldn't like to be in his job -

JEREMY, AGE 9

All he does is just makes laws that he can't keep and then breaks them to make new ones -

FRANK, AGE 9

He is an important man. He makes lots of choices and fights for what he thinks. I would NOT like to be the Prime Minister -

ABI, AGE 10

He gives money to the poor -

GEORGINA, AGE 8

You always see him on telly but I hav

The prime minister does things and stops things that happen -

ANON

The Prime Minister at the moment is making a hash -

LOUISA, AGE 9

The Prime Minister sits around telling people to do this and that for him and gets very angry. I think he is boring -

CLAIRE, AGE 10

The Prime Minister does not do much but talk and shout at people -

EDWARD, AGE 9

ALICE C, AGE 9

He locks people up -
ISABELLE D, AGE 8

The Prime Minister controls all the money and decides where to spend it -
ADAM, AGE 10

All he does is make stupid speeches. I think Nelson Mandeler of Africa is better -
RACHAEL D

They yap and yap -
EMMA H, AGE 7

He does the news on televison -
NICHOLAS H, AGE 8

ever figured out what he does -
MARK, AGE 10

He works day and night -
JAMES, AGE 7

The Prime Minister works out the prices for food -
ROGER, AGE 10

The Prime Minister helps Mr Clinton run Britain -
STEPHEN, AGE 6

He looks after us -
CARL, AGE 7

He sits on a chair on the tv and talks a load of pap -
SHAMI, AGE 10

He says speeches all day and goes to the pub at night -
GLYN M

"Children need love,
especially when they do
not deserve it."

HAROLD HULBERT

What do you think about grandparents?

They are funny, because they hear things wrong -

EMMA C, AGE 8

I don't think much about grandparents -

STEPHEN, AGE 7

They just sit and watch tv -

IAN T

I think grandparents are great, 'cause they had my mum and my mum had me so that's why I'm in this world -

LI-LI, AGE 9

SOPHIE, AGE 7

They are nice, because they look after me. They have got a special cat, he is old, he loves fish. He has had four teeth out -

SARAH, AGE 6

What do you think about grandparents?

They live too far away -
KRISTIAN, AGE 4

They are really mint -
GORDON, AGE 10

Grandparents are quite old-fashioned -
SALLY, AGE 9

Grandparents are nice because they give you sausages, potatoes and peas -
ADAM, AGE 6

They are kand and jentle and loveng -
GEMMA, AGE 7

They are funny, because my grandpa limps and it is funny -
HANNAH, AGE 6

They are kind and understanding -
GEMMA, AGE 10

I think grandparents are quite spectacular and

They really like you and try their best to care for you. I like them -
NICK A, AGE 10

Grandparents are the best people in the world. They give you everything you are not allowed at home -
NINA, AGE 10

I think the world of them -
PETER J, AGE 8

I think about my grandparents as exciting, funny and sleepy -
ROSEANNA HART, AGE 8

Grandparents are really fun when you are playing board games, but they're not very energetic. After all their years, they are sometimes quite good cooks -
ANNA, AGE 10

I like the one in Blackpool, because he had a car crash -

BETH, AGE 6

I like them because they are always there if you need someone to babysit -

CHARLOTTE, AGE 10

I think my alive grandparents are kind, but annoying. My dead ones were kinder than kind -

MICHAEL B

They are old and rinkley -

CAROL, AGE 10

I love my grandparents for what they are -

RACHEL, AGE 10

ometimes I wonder how mine are still alive -

WUNMI A, AGE 10

They are sweet, have curly hair, blue eyes, red lips and red cheeks, and they buy presents -

SARAH SMITH, AGE 6

They are always wanting to know what is going on, but apart from that they are nice -

DEBORAH, AGE 10

Grandparents don't do anything, because they are too old -

JACK, AGE 10

STEPHEN FRASER, AGE 10

"Children are a
poor man's riches."

ANON

What would you do if you won the National Lottery?

I would jump up in joy. Then I would save it for when I get older to buy a nice house and a nice car -

JAY, AGE 11

JACK D, AGE 8

I'd probably scream with happiness knowing that I could buy all the things I have ever wanted, and that's quite a lot of stuff! -

EMMA, AGE 11

Live in Turkey at a bar, because it is hot and there are lots of cocktails and boys -

ELLY, AGE 8

I would buy my school -

ASHRAFUL, AGE 10

If I won the national lottery I would go to my newspaper shop and would ask them for my money -

ALICIA J, AGE 7

I would get a car and a house and a baby and a bike -

JAHED U, AGE 8

I would take my best friend and me to swim with dolphins somewhere -

MARIE, AGE 10

What would you do if you won the National Lottery?

Biyacar -

AARON

I'd go to MacDonalds every lunch time because I hate sandwiches, especially wholegrain, but I'd only eat chicken nuggets and chips so I don't die of BSE. I'd get great big strawberry saucey ice-cream and I'd gobble it down as fast as I could, which would leave my mouth burning and my teeth tingling -

NAOMI, AGE 10

I would go out and buy every pet shop, then pay people to clean them out -

SARAH P, AGE 10

I would get lots of sweets and lots of slush puppies and a stresh limow -

ERIN M

I would buy my own fairground with a giant roller coaster, shop till I drop and buy every pet shop there is -

CLAIRE, AGE 10

I would run down the stree

Go to Barbados and buy a shop in Kent -

SAMANTHA B, AGE 9

If I won the lottery I wouldn't boast that much. Anyway, I can't win the lottery because I don't buy a ticket -

GINNY, AGE 10

I would buy the world's biggest sweet machine and a new Jaguar -

GLYN M

I would buy Alton Towers, Chessington, Turbos the computer shop, all the comics I can, five dogs and a new house -

SCOTT S, AGE 10

I would build a theme park on top of Buckingham Palace -

ALEX, AGE 10

I would first split it between my family and then go clothes shopping for my holiday, which I would take in America and then on to Hawaii and back to Amsterdam, where I would fly back to England and put my left over money (if there was any) in the bank -

EMILY K, AGE 10

I will give half the money to children in need, and live in a mansion with tennis courts and a swimming pool, and Charlie's Chocolate Factory in my back garden -

LUCY, AGE 11

houting "I've won the lottery" -

PAUL, AGE 7

Keep it all in my treasure box -

ERIN, AGE 7

Save it to spend on something -

CHLOË, AGE 7

Buy six Goosebumps books and a leopard -

MATTHEW, AGE 9

I would buy a car, a house, an ice hockey stadium and an ice hockey team -

PAUL, AGE 10

"A kiss, when all is said, what is it?
A rosy dot placed on the 'i' in loving;
'Tis a secret told to the mouth
instead of to the ear."

EDMOND ROSTAND

What do you think about kissing?

If it was with a boy, you'd have to get married -

SARAH SMITH, AGE 6

I don't like it much. It makes my lips sore -

EMMA WILLIAMS, AGE 5

TULLULAH, AGE 8

My mum kisses me all the time and I wipe them off. I don't like them -

CIAN, AGE 4

I love kissing my sister because she is special -

LEO EMMETT, AGE 6

Yuk, because you get other people's germs -

HANNAH-MAY ALMASRY, AGE 6

Personally, I think it is alright if it is just a very quick peck on the cheek -

CATHERINE, AGE 11

It's horrible because your lips feel crunched -

JOHN JAMES CRAWFORD, AGE 6

What do you think about kissing?

It's just a sign that people love each other. I know a girl called Sarah which I quite like, but I would never kiss her -

EMMA, AGE 11

Well, it makes everyone get the tissues out when there is a big smooch at the end of a sad movie, but I think it is nice until tongues get involved -

LIZZIE, AGE 10

It is a normal reaction and sometimes you do it because you love people -

GINNY, AGE 10

Kissing is out of the question -

EMMA, AGE 8

I think it is a very good thin

Kissing is a romantic thing that people do when they are really in love -

MARIE, AGE 10

Kissing is disgusting, but if it is family it is OK (not boys in the family) -

SARA P, AGE 10

Personally, I only like to be kissed by a member of my family. I will probably think differently when I'm older -

KATY, AGE 10

It's all right at the right place at the right time -

SAM, AGE 10

I think kissing is okay if you're over 12 and you have a boyfriend, or if it is your family, but otherwise I think it is revolting -

FRANCESCA R, AGE 9

I think lis a sighn of love.

I think kissing is horrible unless it is with mark owen or paul nicols, then I would never stop -

RACHAEL D

Kissing is smelly madness - unless it is with a supermodel -

ROBERT C

ut I wouldn't like to do it -

AMANDA, AGE 10

What I think about kissing is nothing and sick!!!!!! -

GLYN M

Kissing is most unpleasant -

EDWARD, AGE 9

When you marry people you have to kiss them -

SAMI, AGE 6

Excellent -
MOHAMMED N, AGE 9

I don't mind kissing my mum and dad, but if you are going out with someone, I think it is gross. It is also alright if you are married -

CLAIRE, AGE 10

I think kissing is nice. I kiss my dad when he leaves me at school -

RAHUL I, AGE 5

"It is dangerous
to confuse children
with angels."

DAVID FYFE

What does God do?

He loves us truly -

MICHAEL, AGE 6

I think he is a magician who helps people -

CLAUDIA H, AGE 8

He makes a boat -

OLIVIA, AGE 4

Our father what art in heaven Harold be thy name -

HELEN, AGE 6

He gives us light in the night and the day -

SHAHED, AGE 9

When you go to sleep, he lets you sleep comfortably -

RAJU R, AGE 8

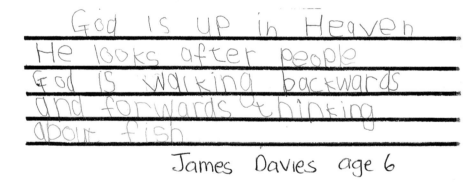

God is up in Heaven
He looks after people
God is walking backwards
and forwards thinking
about fish

James Davies age 6

What does God do? He makes us happy -

ZOË S

He sings -

MILLIE, AGE 4

He looks after the spirits in the air -

YASMIN, AGE 7

What does God do?

God makes things happen -
ELLA F, AGE 8

God makes the wind and the ear and the sun and the rain -
JASMINE

He makes sure our mums keep us alive -
THOMAS PYM, AGE 6

He made all the bugs -
VERITY, AGE 5

God sometimes does the cooking for Jesus -
CATHERINE WIGNALL, AGE 5

Just about everthink -
MELISSA Z

Watches us -
RICHARD, AGE 7

God is flowing in the air an

He makes medecine -
HANNAH-MAY ELMASRY, AGE 6

God lives in heaven and goes round in a spaceship -
JAMES HART, AGE 5

This i

He builds houses -
ELSPETH CLARK, AGE 5

God gives powers to Jesus - nice powers. God is powerful. God looks down on the other people -
CATRIONA TILL, AGE 5

He helps us when we are in trouble -
WILLIAM, AGE 6

He's your friend -
NICK A, AGE 10

He helps people and he sends the sun and rain and he blesses people and has a magic telescope that can see through walls -
EDWIN, AGE 6

God makes his own clothes -
EMMA COX, AGE 5

He sees you if you are being good, and he sends a robin to see, and he tells Father Christmas -
KAREN, AGE 7

God is an ecsuse to go to church -
MATTHEW

He makes the wind when you are flying kites -
SOPHIE, AGE 5

God sits up in heaven smoking a pipe picking out all the people he wants in heaven when they die -
ANON

God is always with you if you are unhappy and need help -
SALLY, AGE 9

God created the world and if he didn't I wouldn't be here -
RYAN, AGE 10

e's next to us at each second -
ROSEANNA HART, AGE 8

ɪod

God listens to people praying and thanking him for the beautiful surroundings and their life. When you need him he always helps you if he can -
ANNA, AGE 10

God makes the food. He makes the bread and fish. God was pleased to see Uncle Philip. Uncle Philip is having a rest. God is waiting at the door for other people -
EMMA WILLIAMS, AGE 5

God listens -
GEMMA, AGE 10

God tempts you to be good and go to boring church with lots of sermons -
RHIANNON, AGE 10

He owns the world -
MAX, AGE 6

Anything he likes -
JENNY L, AGE 9

I don't like God because he hits you when you are naughty -
RAHUL I, AGE 5

"Fame is proof
that people are gullible."

RALPH WALDO EMERSON

Who is your favourite famous person, why do you like them and what would you say to him or her if you met?

Well, there are lots. David Seaman, Dennis Bergkamp, Ian Wright, Paul Merson, and some more Arsenal players, and I would say to them, "Can I have a season ticket?" -
STEPHEN L, AGE 8

My daddy, because he is bringing me a Playmobil thing -
LOUIS, AGE 4

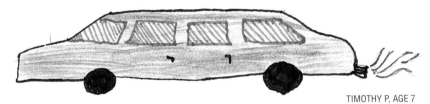

TIMOTHY P, AGE 7

I like the Beatles because they sing good songs. I would say to them, "Would you like to come to lunch?" -
MELANIE W, AGE 8

Everybody on tele -
DAVID JANES, AGE 5

The queen, because every time I visit her she gives me a packet of sweets -
SARAH SMITH, AGE 6

My dad is famous. I like him -
CIAN, AGE 4

Peggy Patch from Playdays because she likes red and I do -
SARAH, AGE 6

Granny -
BECKY, AGE 4

My favourite person is Sam (in my class) because she is lovely -
KEVIN R

My favourite famous person is Piet Mondrian. I like him because he does cubism drawing, and if I met him I would say, "I love your drawings" -
ALICE POTTER, AGE 7

Michael Heseltine, I don't know why -
TOBY, AGE 5

70 | 71

Who is your favourite famous person, why do you like them and what would you say to him or her if you met?

The Queen, because she lets us visit her castle. I would say to her, "Can I have some of your money?" -

LIAM CHAMBERS, AGE 5

My favourite person is Buddy Holly because I love his songs and if I met him I would fall on the floor and faint -

RITA, AGE 10

My favourite famous person is the Queen, and if I saw her I would say thank you for all the lovely things we have -

ROSEANNA HART, AGE 8

I would like to meet Jack Nicholson so I cou

The Bishop of Oxford -

LAURA, AGE 4

I love Elvis Presley and If I met him I would go "Screeeeeeeeeeeeam" -

LOUISE, AGE 9

Robin Hood, because he robbed the rich to feed the poor, and I would say to him, "Can I marry you?" -

REBECCA, AGE 5

My favourite person is my teddy, because he smiles at me -

YASMIN B, AGE 5

ell him " I have got the same name as you " -

JACK NICHOLSON, AGE 10

My favourite person is a man from Bangaladesh. His name is Cazi Nozrool Eslam, he is a great poet. I really like his poems in Bengali, they rhyme and are always told nicely, but now he's dead, but if I met him I would like a picture of him and his autograph and I would ask him if he would write one of his best poems ever -

SALMAN O

I think it has to be Eric Cantona. I like him because he is a very good footballer and if I met him I would say, "Can you come and play for the Arsenal?" -

WUNMI A, AGE 10

"Nothing is so
firmly believed as what
we least know."

MICHAEL DE MONTAIGNE

None of the children had difficulty answering this question… but several said they did not believe in God.

What is a real fairy like?

They have wings, a pink dress and a magic wand -
SARAH SMITH, AGE 6

Goldy-yellow like a pixie. I saw a pixie on my roof. It didn't say anything because it thought I was asleep -
EMMA WILLIAMS, AGE 5

KATIE L, AGE 9

What is a real fairy like?

White dress and yellowy-golden hair. Granny saw a fairy near Portmadoc skipping over the wall -

EMMA COX, AGE 6

Pink dress with a blue bow. Quite small with blonde hair -

PHOEBE BALL, AGE 5

ANNA, AGE

It has purple wings

A lovely mum -

EMMA B

Small, pretty, with wings. I think I have seen one - but I can't quite remember. Or was it my imagination? -

JAMES DAVIES, AGE 6

Like us but smaller. You can have baby fairies and old ones -

CATRIONA TILL, AGE 5

I dress up as Tinkerbell. I have silver top and a pink shirt with stars on and a little crown. I have magic wand -

ELIZABETH ASHBY, AGE 5

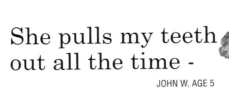

She pulls my teeth out all the time -

JOHN W, AGE 5

DANIEL, AGE 7

nd a blue magic wand -

HARRY WROUGHTON-CRAIG, AGE 5

He has a wand and wings and a round thing -

PATRICK Q, AGE 6

A fairy is light, pretty, little clothes, very, very small, wears a white dress and is small, kind, helpful, tiny, funny, nice, pretty and magic and pretty -

JANEY, AGE 7

"A wise scepticism
is the first attribute of
a good critic."

JAMES RUSSELL LOWELL

What is Britain best at?

Expensive houses -
OLIVER H, AGE 7

WE ARE THE CHAMPIONS

BRITAIN IS BEST

I ♥ U

Mrs Nodge is a Nugget

LOUISE L, AGE 9

Looking after pets -
CLAUDIA H, AGE 8

Britain is not best at football -
ROSEANNA HART, AGE 8

Fighting the Romans -
SEBASTIAN, AGE 6

Writing -
HUGH, AGE 6

Having a lot of toy shops to get toys from -
EMMA D, AGE 8

Roller-skating -
SOFIE, AGE 6

What is Britain best at?

Rain -
PETER, AGE 8

Talking and
sleeping -
BETH, AGE 6

Catching stupids of
the IRA -
BENJAMIN, AGE 8

Catching mad cow
disease -
LESLEY J

They used to be good at cric

Fiting, grifite, swering,
stiling -
GORDON, AGE 10

Britain is best at having a nut as the prime
minister -
MICHAEL B

Britain is best at
having good
programmes on
television -
ROSIE, AGE 8

Britain is best at
the paralympics -
GAETAN, AGE 10

Britain is best at making not very
good quality things, but a lot of the
people are friendly and kind -

ANNA, AGE 10

Britain is good at
some things, like
sport (well, not
that good) -

SHAHEDA B

et, but now they are not -

HUGO, AGE 6

Fish and chips -

WUNMI A, AGE 10

Growing apples-

LAUREN F

"Distance is a great promoter of admiration."

DENIS DIDEROT

What is the best country in the world, and why?

The best country is Spain, because I like the way they talk -

ANON

The best country in the world is Ghana, because it is hot absolutely every day, even if it is raining -

ANITA A, AGE 10

Japan, because I can spell it right -

JAMIE, AGE 7

Scotland is the best country in the world, because it is always warm and has lots of friendly animals -

ISABELLE D, AGE 8

It is our garden, because it has tree houses -

JAMES, AGE 7

Egypt, because of all the 3-D pyramids -

SARAH H, AGE 9

The best country is America, because it has got Seaworld, and four more things -

JACK, AGE 7

New Zeled, because my old teachers lives there and they said it is sometimes sunny -

USFO B

Every year I go to the Caribbean, to a place called Lanzarote, and that would have to be the best romantic place in the world. In a restaurant I was going to the toilet, and my dad put a chilley in my ice cream and I et it and my mouth was spicey for two weeks -

JEREMY, AGE 9

What is the best country in the world, and why?

The best country must be Africa, because it's nice and hot and doesn't rain much, unlike Scarborough -

SARA, AGE 11

Nigeria - it's got dogs and chickens -

AYODELE A, AGE 9

Mauritius, because it has got nice water and it is clean -

RYAN F

Theydon Bois -

ASHRAFUL, AGE 10

The best country in the world is Italy, because I absolutely love spaghetti -

MARIE L, AGE 10

The best country in the world is Disney La

England, because it is an island -

JONATHAN, AGE 10

My favourite country must be China. I've never been there, but if we ate the food I'd be happy - squiggling the noodles one strip at a time, and gobbling down the sweet and sours, with it all around my face -

NAOMI, AGE 10

My home is the best country in the world and I would HATE to live anywhere else, even paradise -

CLAIRE, AGE 10

The best is Einglund. I like it becose there is lots of countrys in it -

PETER, AGE 7

The best country is France, because there is good food, no bad spiders and the weather is good, but only the south. I have never been to France -

JOE, AGE 11

The best country in the world is Italy, because some of the greatest artists and composers started there and there are some lovely cities and buildings -

EMILY, AGE 10

England, because I am used to it, and I haven't been to any others -

NATALIE, AGE 8

Bangaladesh, because it is sunny -

SHOAFADA, AGE 7

...ause all the cartoon characters live there -

JOSHUA, AGE 10

America is my favourite, because everything is just at hand -

ADAM, AGE 10

Wales, because there is always sun and the accents are nice -

ZOEY M

England, because it has got nice clothes -

LUCKY K, AGE 9

"At Christmas play and
make good cheer, for Christmas
comes but once a year."

THOMAS TUSSER

Why do we have Christmas?

So mummies don't have to
waste money on toys -

EMMA WILLIAMS, AGE 5

GRACE D, AGE 7

To get more
presents -

NATASHA, AGE 4

We just do -

LOUIS, AGE 4

Why do we have Christmas?

Because it is important, otherwise you would run out of things. So you must have Father Christmas -

ANNA JAMES, AGE 5

To celebrate my rabbit's birthday -

ALICE, AGE 5

So the mummies and daddies don

To celebrate my birthday -

OLIVER, AGE 5

To remind us all to love each other -

STEVEN, AGE 6

Because it is Jesus's birthday -

SAM, AGE 7

Mum throws away your old toys and you can get some news ones -

JONJO, AGE 6

ave to buy you presents -

THOMAS, AGE 5

If you didn't, you would only get presents on your birthday -

EMMA, AGE 8

SALLIE E, AGE 7

"Nature fits
all her children with
something to do."

JAMES RUSSELL LOWELL

What should we do to make the world better?

To make the world better, I think cigarettes should be a hundred pounds -

EMMA D, AGE 8

We have to stop tellings tails -

MELANIE W, AGE 8

I pick up the rubbish off the street to make the paths clean for everybody.

Make the world happy. Sing a song -

HARRY WROUGHTON-CRAIG, AGE 5

Don't hunt, and put things in the bin -

ELLA F, AGE 8

What should we do to make the world better?

Stop everything nasty happening -
SEBASTIAN, AGE 6

Pay the mums and dads more cash -
BETH, AGE 6

Give poor people enough money to buy food -
SALMAN O

Build roads and shops -
KATY, AGE 5

Me and my friends pick flowers in the field for each other. It makes me feel happy -
SARAH SMITH, AGE 6

Don't have any wars, give money to the homeless and poor. Also give more money for schools instead of giving the money to build golf courses. Schools need it more for children to learn, as you did when you were at school -
LUCY, AGE 11

I would put up lots of

Writing -
HUGH, AGE 6

Give it bananas -
MARK P, AGE 6

Look after the world and not drop litter -
REBECCA, AGE 7

To make the world better, all the automobiles should run on electricity -
GAETAN, AGE 10

Build more space shuttles, because I want to go to space -
MATTHEW A, AGE 9

Be tidy and expesherly throw chewing gum in the bin because dogs can get it on their foot -

MELISSA Z

Nothing. It is all right -

MICHELLE, AGE 7

Get rid of all the horrible people like robbers and kidnappers -

ANNA, AGE 10

If we drop rubbish on the floor we should pick it up, or get more caretakers -

SABIA K

Ban smoking, joy-riding and drinking -

RACHEL, AGE 10

Stop spitting on the floor -

HUMAYUN, AGE 6

osters saying do not ploot -

SOPHIE L, AGE 7

Have no school, but be taught at home -

ALICE, AGE 10

Give everybody some medecine -

HANMORE, AGE 5

Stop people from carrying knives -

SAMANTHA, AGE 10

Fix it -

NABIL M

I think to make the world better we should keep it hygenic. I'm not trying to be bad to people who love cars, but I don't think we should have any, just for the sake of animals and our health. We should stop air pollution and drop our rubbish in the bin. As we all say, it's a small world -

WUNMI A, AGE 10

Do magic -

BETH, AGE 7

"Now tell us all about the war,
and what they fought each other for."

ROBERT SOUTHEY

What are wars?

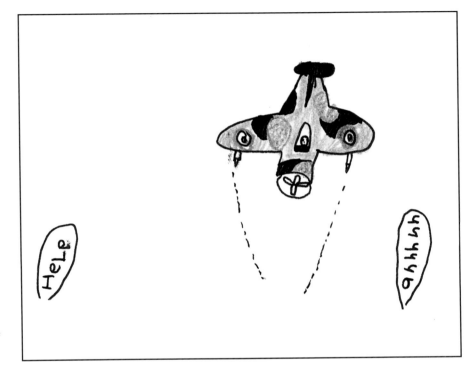

Fighting about money.
They use swords -

EMMA WILLIAMS, AGE 5

I think they are horrid things, wars, with
persecution, despising, and no doubt, some
nasty leaders -

ALICE MALIN, AGE 7

People fight and they fall
over -

SOPHIE EVANS, AGE 5

A war is fighting
between two or
more sort of teams -

OLIVER, AGE 8

They are fighting, and violent, and that is
even worse -

JACK, AGE 7

It is where people
disagree and start
a fight. This fight
turns into a battle
and this involves
weapons, which
becomes a WAR -

EMMA, AGE 11

What are wars?

A war is something when one man leads one country to conker another and you have to fight if you are a reasonable age -

JOE, AGE 11

A load of useless bangs, booms and smashes for no reason, and it never gets anyone anywhere -

LIZZIE, AGE 10

Wars are when people go and annoy themselves and everybody else by killing each other. They ruin countries and people's feelings -

CATHERINE, AGE 11

Wars are when two or even three countries are fighting to take over anot

In the last war Britain fought the Nancies -

SOPHIE L, AGE 7

There are wars when my sister decides to sing -

ALEX, AGE 10

Wars are terrible fights like me and my brother have sometimes -

ALICE M

Wars are things that start when Prime Ministers argue -

CRAIG, AGE 10

Wars are started by a disagreement and innocent people end up getting seriously hurt or killed. I think wars are started by immature decisions made by people who should just sit down and work it out instead of bringing innocent people into it -

JEMMA H, AGE 10

When the Germans fight the English -

LEWIS, AGE 6

Wars are when people have humungous tomato fights -

BILL, AGE 10

Who doesn't win has a nice grave and a cross nearby -

POSIE, AGE 7

ntry. There was the first world war, the second world war, and the golf war -

CLAIRE, AGE 10

Wars are Vikings with daggers -

SAMI, AGE 6

Wars are big arguments that are even worse than me and my brother, and that has got to be bad -

LORRAINE B

They are about good and evil -

MICHAEL, AGE 6

Wars are when you want to do something back to someone -

CHLOË, AGE 6

"I would not be a queen
for all the world."

WILLIAM SHAKESPEARE (KING HENRY VIII)

What does the Queen do?

She does a wicked spell on her friends -

LUCY, AGE 4

She sings -

TOM, AGE 4

The quine keeps on kissing prins chalrs -

MARC, AGE 7

She bakes in the kitchen -

HARRY WROUGHTON-CRAIG, AGE 5

The queen roams around the country -

MATTHEW L

She does nothing -

ADAM, AGE 6

The queen writes letters to the Mayor
The Queen writes letters to the Mayor
she has a purple pen

Emma Cox
age 6.

She waves -

RUMI B, AGE 8

She looks after the world -

SOFIE, AGE 6

What does the Queen do?

The Queen tries to make everyone happy. But I don't think she is doing a very good job -

FAYMA

Eats jaffa cakes and goes back to bed -

PATRICK Q, AGE 5

She just sits back and lets her servants do all the dirty work -

ASHLEY, AGE 8

The Queen goes on televison to talk about her holidays. She stays in a hotel in Wales for a few days -

CATRIONA TILL, AGE 5

The Queen dives in her pool of money. She swims in the money -

GEORGE BRERETON, AGE 5

The Queen looks after her baby girl called Topsy. The Queen rocks Topsy to sleep -

PHOEBE BALL, AGE 5

She sends you

She drives around in her ruals roys all day -

CLAIRE S, AGE 7

She has people around for supper and she dresses in her finest clothes and dances in the ballroom -

BETH, AGE 6

The Queen walks around looking for gold. The King helps her -

LIAM CHAMBERS, AGE 5

She gets all the best food -

GWILYM, AGE 7

The Queen eats peas, fish fingers and mashed potatoes. She wears rubber gloves to wash up in the sink -

SARAH SMITH, AGE 6

All she does is wave her hand and count her money, and is posh -

RHIANNON D

She reads a book and sometimes has a nap-

SION, AGE 6

The queen loves us, cares for us and lazes around and has servants -

ROSEANNA HART, AGE 8

She is wicked -

CAMILLA, AGE 5

Orders people to get her cups of tea -

HAYLEY, AGE 6

She sees everyone when you be naughty and she writes in her book -

MUBIN, AGE 6

The Queen asks the King questions, and writes thank you letters for presents -

RHYS W, AGE 6

our passport -

KATE, AGE 6

The queen is a very rich person, and all I ever see her doing is getting out of planes in foreign countries -

ANNA, AGE 10

She plays with her jewellery -

CHRISTIE M

She goes to see *Dragonheart* at the cinema -

REISS A, AGE 5

The Queen sit's on her thron with her cron on with her cup of tea -

JASMINE

"Trifles make perfection,
and perfection is no trifle."

MICHELANGELO

What would you like to do to have your absolutely perfect day?

Go to the zoo with all the teachers, and they get eaten by a lion -

SCOTT, AGE 10

Go swimming or go to hardford cher -

RYAN F

I would go to space -

JAMES, AGE 7

Have Sam not pestering me -

JACK, AGE 7

It would have to be learning to drive, because it would give me extra freedom -

SAM, AGE 11

AMY

My perfect day would be my wedding day. I am not going to tell you who I would like to get married to, but I would have everyone I ever liked there -

EMMA, AGE 11

What would you like to do to have your absolutely perfect day?

I'd like to be off school with no dancing, no guides, nothing. And I'd like to be playing and having fun with my friends, or go with a friend somewhere nice and hot where my brother isn't there or my mum, dad or sister. Where nobody was there to bother me -

MARIE, AGE 10

I'd like to go to Florida, lay in a hammock between two palm trees and drink lemonade, soaking up the sun, occasionally having a swim -

SAM, AGE 10

I would go to the beach for the whole day with some friends, and when I go home have a big barbecue -

AMANDA, AGE 10

Go to Saf end -

ALEX B

I would like to sleep all day long watchir

To see my mum have a baby boy -

JENNY, AGE 10

For my perfect day, I would go to a park -

ALICIA J, AGE 7

Win the lottery, and have my mum and dad get together again -

CHRISTOPHER, AGE 11

Play outside -

SHAHAN A, AGE 8

Buy a box of chocolates and eat them all by myself -

NURYA S, AGE 11

Go to Australia to watch the grand prix and meet Damon Hill and get a private tour of the Williams team -

JERRY, AGE 10

The way to have a perfect day with me is to have Neon Nerds for every meal at Disneyworld and go on all the rides free -

GWILYM, AGE 7

My perfect day would be going to MacDonalds on Christmas day and winning the lottery that night -

ABI, AGE 10

Be a good boy -

SIMON, AGE 6

Perform in a fairly big concert and raise money for charity -

ALICE, AGE 10

and having slaves to do my work -

MARIE L, AGE 10

I'd go fishing, catch loads of big fish and sell them and go to the theme park and then go to Wimpeys and then get drunk -

PETER, AGE 6

First do maths, then some drawing, then play, then do writing, then read, then have lunch, then do art -

EMMA, AGE 8

Go swimming, go to Brazil and Spain and get a garden with a big house -

BARRY H

Have an apple, and be good -

KOLBEINN M, AGE 6

"Examinations are formidable even to the best prepared..."

C.C. COLTON.

Exams. A slip of the pen, a moment's aberration - exam invigilators tell it like it is...

When men went to fight in the wars, their wives were left alone and that caused havoc because they tarted about, causing the population to rise.

What proportion of the Earth's surface is covered by sea?
The blue bits.

Farmers keep pigs to manicure the fields.

The pill is easy to use and very useful for an eager woman.

A 60 foot tree can break wind for up to 200 yards.

Eskimos are unusual people. Every few years they jump into the sea and swim and swim until they drown. No-one knows why they do this.

How are the buildings in San Francisco built to be safe from earthquakes?
1) They build rubber buildings.
2) The buildings don't quite touch the ground.

A polygon with seven sides is called a hooligan.

The bees were bizzine in the rosy dandrum tree. The little birds wer tittering in the trees.

HATTIE, AGE 5

Trigonometry is when a lady marries three men at the same time.

Saliva is what you ge

The process of filtration makes water safer for drinking because it removes large pollutants like grit, sand, dead sheep, and canoeists.

People should not serve food in shops if they are deceased in any way.

For a nosebleed: Put the nose much lower then the body until the heart stops.

A major disease associated with smoking is death.

A weather saying - Red sky at night, Turkish Delight.

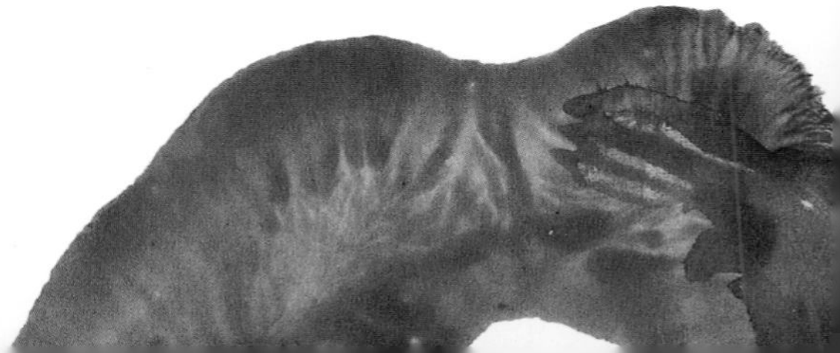

Our father who art in heaven, hello what's your name.

If one angle of a triangle is more than 90 degrees, the triangle is obscene.

The Prime Minister has the power to appoint and disappoint members of the Cabinet.

The moon is a planet just like the earth, only it is even deader

ff the top of a volcano.

What is the difference between how salmon have babies and how humans have babies?
Humans go to hospital.

KATIE, AGE 5

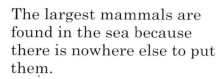

The largest mammals are found in the sea because there is nowhere else to put them.

Food is in the colon and semicolon.

Herbicides are plants

Involuntary muscles are not as willing as voluntary ones.

Dear Sir, Bobby has not come to school because he has got rabies again.

A fossil is an extinct animal. The older it is, the more extinct it is.

A magnet is something you find in a bad apple.

Children were born every year in the 18th century.

Seals stay on the ground and lay their eggs there because there are no trees to go and lay their eggs in.

In a partnership the sleeping partners wake up when the profits are going to be shared out.

When does Britain get most of its rain?
Sundays.

hat eat their young.

Who led the invasion of England in 1066? Victor the Viking.

MITCHELL, AGE 6

EMMA WILLIAMS, AGE 5